THE ~~COMPLETE~~

GRANDMA

RECIPES

COOKBOOK

GRANDMA'S TIMELESS RECIPES

JAMES M. DUSTIN

TABLE OF CONTENT

ABOUT GRANDMA RECIPES COOKBOOK

Embark on a culinary journey through the pages of the Grandma Recipes Cookbook, where the art of cooking meets the warmth of cherished traditions.

This bountiful collection not only unveils a treasure trove of delectable recipes but also captures the heart and soul of generations past.

With each turn of the page, savor the rich flavors and timeless stories that make this cookbook a culinary masterpiece, preserving the magic of Grandma's kitchen for generations to come.

THE CULINARY LEGACY OF GRANDMAS

Creating a **"Grandma recipes cookbook"** is a wonderful way to preserve culinary legacies. Include cherished family recipes, anecdotes, and perhaps some photos to capture the essence of each dish and the memories associated with them.

TIPS FOR COOKING LIKE GRANDMA

1. Classic Ingredients: Use traditional, high-quality ingredients like real butter, fresh herbs, and farm-fresh produce for an authentic flavor.

2. Slow Cooking: Embrace slow-cooking methods like simmering stews, roasting meats, and slow-baking to enhance flavors and create tender dishes.

3. Handwritten Recipes: Consider including handwritten recipes with personal notes, giving the cookbook a nostalgic touch.

4. Family Stories: Share anecdotes and stories related to the recipes, connecting the dishes to family memories for a richer experience.

5. Comfort Food: Grandma's recipes often focus on comfort. Include hearty, comforting dishes that evoke warmth and familiarity.

6. Seasonal Cooking: Highlight the importance of cooking with seasonal ingredients, aligning with the way Grandma may have adapted recipes based on what was available.

7. Preserving Techniques: If applicable, include recipes or tips on preserving foods, as this was often a skill passed down through generations.

8. Simple Techniques: Grandma's recipes often relied on straightforward techniques. Break down complicated steps into simple, easy-to-follow instructions.

9. Family Traditions: Incorporate recipes that were staples during family gatherings or holidays, emphasizing the role of food in family traditions.

10. Homemade Goodies: Include recipes for homemade jams, pickles, and baked goods. These are often treasures in Grandma's repertoire.

11. Attention to Detail: Encourage attention to detail, such as precise measurements and careful preparation, to capture the essence of Grandma's meticulous cooking style.

12. Generosity in Portions: Grandma's cooking often meant hearty portions. Provide guidance on adapting recipes for larger gatherings or leftovers.

CHAPTER 1

BREAKFAST DELIGHTS

FLUFFY PANCAKES

- *Serving Size: 4 servings*

- *Prep Time: 10 minutes*

- *Cooking Time: 10 minutes*

Nutrition Info (per serving):
- Calories: 250
- Protein: 7g
- Fat: 10g
- Carbohydrates: 32g
- Fiber: 1g
- Sugar: 7g
- Sodium: 580mg

Ingredients:
- 1 cup all-purpose flour
- 2 tablespoons sugar
- 1 tablespoon baking powder
- 1/2 teaspoon salt
- 1 cup milk
- 1 large egg
- 2 tablespoons melted butter

- 1 teaspoon vanilla extract

Directions:

1. In a large mixing bowl, whisk together the flour, sugar, baking powder, and salt.

2. In a separate bowl, beat the egg and then add the milk, melted butter, and vanilla extract. Mix well.

3. Pour the wet ingredients into the dry ingredients and gently stir until just combined. Be careful not to overmix; a few lumps are okay.

4. Heat a griddle or non-stick skillet over medium heat. Lightly grease the surface with cooking spray or a small amount of butter.

5. For each pancake, ladle about 1/4 cup of batter onto the griddle. Cook until bubbles form on the surface, then flip and cook the other side until golden brown.

6. Repeat until all the batter is used, adjusting the heat if necessary to prevent burning.

7. Serve the pancakes warm with your favorite toppings, such as maple syrup, fresh berries, or whipped cream.

VEGGIE OMELETTE

- *Serving Size: 1 omelette*

- *Cooking Time: 10 minutes*

- *Prep Time: 5 minutes*

Nutrition Info:
Approximately 250 calories per serving

Ingredients:
- **2 large eggs**
- **1/4 cup diced bell peppers (mix of colors)**
- **1/4 cup diced tomatoes**
- **1/4 cup chopped spinach**
- **2 tablespoons diced onions**
- **1/4 cup shredded cheese (optional)**
- **Salt and pepper to taste**
- **1 tablespoon olive oil**

Directions:

1. Prep Veggies:
   - Dice bell peppers, tomatoes, and onions. Chop spinach.

2. Whisk Eggs:
   - In a bowl, whisk eggs until well beaten. Add a pinch of salt and pepper.

3. Heat Pan:
   - Heat olive oil in a non-stick skillet over medium heat.

4. Sauté Veggies:
   - Sauté onions until translucent, then add bell peppers and tomatoes. Cook until veggies are tender. Add spinach and cook until wilted.

5. Pour Eggs:
   - Pour the whisked eggs over the sautéed veggies in the skillet.

6. Swirl and Cook:
   - Swirl the pan to spread the eggs evenly. Allow the edges to set, lifting them slightly to let the uncooked eggs flow underneath.

7. Add Cheese (Optional):
   - If desired, sprinkle shredded cheese over one half of the omelette.

8. Fold and Serve:
   - Once the eggs are set but still slightly runny on top, fold the omelette in half using a spatula.

9. Finish Cooking:
   - Cook for an additional 1-2 minutes until the cheese is melted, and the omelette is cooked through but still moist.

10. Serve Warm:

- Slide the Veggie Omelette onto a plate and serve immediately.

Nutrition Tips:
- This Veggie Omelette is a rich source of protein, vitamins, and minerals.
- Feel free to customize with your favorite veggies or herbs for added flavor and nutrition.
- Opt for whole eggs for a boost of healthy fats and additional nutrients.

AVOCADO TOAST WITH POACHED EGG

- *Prep Time: 10 minutes*

- *Cooking Time: 10 minutes*

- *Serving Size: 2*

Nutrition Information (per serving):
- **Calories: 350**
- **Protein: 14g**
- **Fat: 20g**
- **Carbohydrates: 30g**
- **Fiber: 10g**

Ingredients:
- **1 ripe avocado**

- 2 slices of whole-grain bread
- 2 large eggs
- Salt and pepper to taste
- Optional toppings: red pepper flakes, chia seeds, or feta cheese

Directions:

1. Avocado Prep:
   - Peel and pit the ripe avocado.
   - Mash the avocado in a bowl, adding salt and pepper to taste.

2. Toast the Bread:
   - Toast two slices of whole-grain bread until golden and crispy.

3. Poach the Eggs:
   - Bring a pot of water to a gentle simmer.
   - Crack each egg into a small bowl.
   - Create a gentle whirlpool in the simmering water and carefully slide the eggs in one at a time.
   - Poach for about 3-4 minutes for a soft, runny yolk.
   - Remove the poached eggs with a slotted spoon and place them on a paper towel to drain excess water.

4. Assembly:
   - Spread the mashed avocado evenly on each slice of toasted bread.
   - Carefully place a poached egg on top of each avocado-covered toast.

5. Optional Toppings:
   - Get creative with additional toppings like red pepper flakes, chia seeds, or crumbled feta cheese.

6. Serve and Enjoy:
   - Your perfect avocado toast with a poached egg is ready to be served! Enjoy this delicious and nutritious meal that's packed with healthy fats, protein, and fiber.

SMOKED SALMON BAGEL

- *Serving Size: 2*

- *Cooking Time: 10 minutes*

- *Prep Time: 15 minutes*

Nutrition Info (per serving):
- **Calories: 400**
- **Protein: 22g**
- **Fat: 18g**
- **Carbohydrates: 40g**
- **Fiber: 4g**

Ingredients:
- **2 bagels (your choice of flavor)**
- **150g smoked salmon**

- 1/2 cup cream cheese
- 1 tablespoon capers
- 1/4 red onion, thinly sliced
- 1 tablespoon fresh dill, chopped
- Lemon wedges for serving
- Salt and pepper to taste

Directions:

1. Preheat the Oven: Toast the bagels in a toaster or preheat your oven to 350°F (175°C).

2. Prepare Toppings: Thinly slice the red onion, chop the fresh dill, and measure out the capers.

3. Spread Cream Cheese: Once the bagels are toasted, spread a generous layer of cream cheese on each half.

4. Layer Smoked Salmon: Divide the smoked salmon evenly between the bagel halves, placing it on top of the cream cheese.

5. Add Toppings: Sprinkle sliced red onion, capers, and fresh dill over the smoked salmon.

6. Season to Taste: Add a pinch of salt and pepper to taste.

7. Serve with Lemon Wedges: Accompany your smoked salmon bagels with lemon wedges for a zesty touch.

CHAPTER 2

SOUPS AND STEWS

MINESTRONE SOUP

- Serving Size: This recipe yields approximately 6 servings.

- Prep Time: Around 15 minutes

- Cooking Time: Approximately 30 minutes

Nutrition Info (per serving):
- **Calories: 250**
- **Protein: 10g**
- **Carbohydrates: 45g**
- **Fat: 4g**
- **Fiber: 8g**

Ingredients:
- 1 tablespoon olive oil
- 1 onion, diced
- 2 carrots, sliced
- 2 celery stalks, chopped
- 3 cloves garlic, minced
- 1 can (15 oz) diced tomatoes
- 1 can (15 oz) kidney beans, drained and rinsed
- 1 can (15 oz) cannellini beans, drained and rinsed

- 6 cups vegetable broth
- 1 cup small pasta (e.g., ditalini or small shells)
- 1 teaspoon dried oregano
- 1 teaspoon dried basil
- 1/2 teaspoon thyme
- Salt and pepper to taste
- 2 cups chopped spinach or kale
- Grated Parmesan cheese for serving

Directions:

1. In a large pot, heat the olive oil over medium heat. Add the diced onion, carrots, celery, and garlic. Sauté until the vegetables are softened.

2. Pour in the diced tomatoes, kidney beans, cannellini beans, and vegetable broth. Stir in the oregano, basil, thyme, salt, and pepper. Bring the soup to a boil, then reduce the heat and let it simmer for about 15 minutes.

3. Add the pasta and continue simmering until the pasta is cooked al dente, following the package instructions.

4. Stir in the chopped spinach or kale and cook until wilted. Adjust the seasoning if necessary.

5. Once ready, ladle the Minestrone soup into bowls and serve with a sprinkle of grated Parmesan cheese on top.

CHICKEN NOODLE SOUP

- *Serving Size: 6 servings*

- *Prep Time: 15 minutes*

- *Cooking Time: 30 minutes*

Nutrition Info (per serving):
- Calories: 250
- Protein: 20g
- Fat: 8g
- Carbohydrates: 22g
- Fiber: 3g

Ingredients:
- 1 pound boneless, skinless chicken breasts, diced
- 8 cups chicken broth
- 3 carrots, sliced
- 3 celery stalks, chopped
- 1 medium onion, finely diced
- 3 cloves garlic, minced
- 2 teaspoons dried thyme
- 2 bay leaves
- Salt and pepper to taste
- 2 cups egg noodles
- Fresh parsley for garnish

Directions:

1. Prepare Ingredients: Chop carrots, celery, onion, and garlic. Dice chicken into bite-sized pieces.

2. Sauté Aromatics: In a large pot, sauté onion and garlic until fragrant. Add chicken and cook until browned.

3. Add Vegetables: Stir in carrots and celery. Sauté for a few minutes until vegetables begin to soften.

4. Seasoning: Season with thyme, salt, and pepper. Toss in bay leaves for added flavor.

5. Simmer: Pour in chicken broth and bring the mixture to a boil. Reduce heat, cover, and simmer for 15-20 minutes until vegetables are tender.

6. Cook Noodles: Meanwhile, cook egg noodles according to package instructions. Drain and set aside.

7. Combine: Add cooked noodles to the soup pot. Adjust seasoning if needed. Simmer for an additional 5 minutes to allow flavors to meld.

8. Serve: Ladle the steaming chicken noodle soup into bowls. Garnish with fresh parsley.

BEEF STEW

- *Serving Size: 6-8 servings*

- *Prep Time: 20 minutes*

- *Cooking Time: 2.5-3 hours*

Nutrition Info (per serving):
- Calories: ~400
- Protein: ~30g
- Carbohydrates: ~30g
- Fat: ~15g
- Fiber: ~5g

Ingredients:
- 2 pounds stew beef, cut into bite-sized chunks
- 4 cups beef broth
- 1 cup red wine (optional)
- 1 large onion, diced
- 3 cloves garlic, minced
- 4 carrots, sliced
- 4 potatoes, diced
- 2 cups celery, chopped
- 1 cup frozen peas
- 2 tablespoons tomato paste
- 1 teaspoon dried thyme
- 2 bay leaves
- Salt and pepper to taste
- 2 tablespoons vegetable oil
- 1/4 cup all-purpose flour for coating

1. In a large bowl, toss the stew beef with flour until evenly coated. In a Dutch oven or large pot, heat vegetable oil over medium-high heat. Brown the beef on all sides. Remove and set aside.

2. In the same pot, sauté onions until translucent. Add garlic and cook for an additional minute. Stir in tomato paste and cook for another 2 minutes.

3. Pour in the red wine (if using) to deglaze the pot, scraping up any browned bits from the bottom. Allow the wine to simmer for a few minutes.

4. Return the browned beef to the pot and add beef broth, thyme, bay leaves, salt, and pepper. Bring to a boil, then reduce heat, cover, and simmer for 1.5 to 2 hours or until the beef is tender.

5. Add carrots, potatoes, celery, and peas to the pot. Simmer for an additional 30 minutes or until the vegetables are cooked through.

6. Adjust seasoning if necessary and discard the bay leaves.

LENTIL SOUP

- *Prep Time: 15 minutes*

- *Cooking Time: 30-40 minutes*

- *Serving Size: 4-6 servings*

Nutrition Information (per serving):

- Calories: 250
- Protein: 15g
- Fat: 6g
- Carbohydrates: 35g
- Fiber: 12g
- Sugar: 5g

Ingredients:

- 1 cup dry green or brown lentils
- 1 onion, diced
- 2 carrots, chopped
- 2 celery stalks, sliced
- 3 cloves garlic, minced
- 1 can (14 oz) diced tomatoes
- 6 cups vegetable or chicken broth
- 1 teaspoon cumin
- 1 teaspoon coriander
- 1 teaspoon smoked paprika

- Salt and pepper to taste
- 2 tablespoons olive oil
- Fresh parsley for garnish (optional)

Directions:

1. Rinse Lentils: Start by rinsing the lentils under cold water and set them aside.

2. Sauté Vegetables: In a large pot, heat olive oil over medium heat. Sauté diced onion, carrots, celery, and minced garlic until the vegetables are tender.

3. Add Spices: Sprinkle cumin, coriander, smoked paprika, salt, and pepper over the sautéed vegetables. Stir well to coat the vegetables with the aromatic spices.

4. Incorporate Lentils and Tomatoes: Add the rinsed lentils, diced tomatoes (with juice), and broth to the pot. Bring the mixture to a boil, then reduce the heat to simmer. Cover the pot and let it cook for 25-30 minutes or until lentils are tender.

5. Adjust Seasoning: Taste the soup and adjust the seasoning if necessary. You can add more salt, pepper, or spices to suit your preference.

6. Serve: Ladle the hot lentil soup into bowls, and if desired, garnish with fresh parsley for a burst of color and added freshness.

TOM YUM SOUP

- *Serving Size: This recipe serves approximately 4 people.*

- *Prep Time: 15 minutes*

- *Cooking Time: 20 minutes*

Nutrition Info (per serving):

- **Calories: 150**
- **Protein: 15g**
- **Fat: 2g**
- **Carbohydrates: 18g**
- **Fiber: 3g**
- **Sugars: 7g**

Ingredients:

- **4 cups of chicken or vegetable broth**
- **1 stalk of lemongrass, bruised**
- **3 kaffir lime leaves**
- **200g (7 oz) shrimp, peeled and deveined**
- **200g (7 oz) mushrooms, sliced**
- **1 medium-sized tomato, cut into wedges**
- **1 small onion, sliced**
- **2-3 bird's eye chilies, crushed**

- 3 tablespoons fish sauce
- 2 tablespoons lime juice
- 1 teaspoon sugar
- Fresh cilantro leaves for garnish

Directions:

1. Prepare Ingredients: Start by cleaning and preparing all your ingredients. Slice the lemongrass, crush the chilies, and slice the mushrooms, tomato, and onion.

2. Simmer the Broth: In a pot, bring the chicken or vegetable broth to a simmer. Add the lemongrass and kaffir lime leaves, allowing them to infuse the broth with their flavors.

3. *Add Vegetables:* Add the sliced mushrooms, tomato wedges, and onion to the simmering broth. Let them cook until they are slightly tender.

4. Introduce Seafood: Drop in the shrimp and cook until they turn pink and opaque. Be careful not to overcook the shrimp to maintain their juiciness.

5. Season the Soup: Stir in the crushed chilies, fish sauce, lime juice, and sugar. Adjust the seasoning according to your taste preferences, adding more fish sauce for saltiness or lime juice for extra acidity.

6. Serve: Once the shrimp are fully cooked, discard the lemongrass and kaffir lime leaves. Ladle the Tom Yum Soup

into bowls, ensuring each serving has a good mix of shrimp, vegetables, and broth.

GAZPACHO

- *Serving Size: 4*

- *Prep Time: 15 minutes*

- *Cooking Time: 0 minutes (Chilling time: 2 hours)*

Nutrition Information (per serving):

- Calories: 180
- Total Fat: 12g
- Saturated Fat: 2g
- Cholesterol: 0mg
- Sodium: 650mg
- Total Carbohydrates: 18g
- Dietary Fiber: 4g
- Sugars: 10g
- Protein: 3g

Ingredients:

- 6 ripe tomatoes, chopped
- 1 cucumber, peeled and diced
- 1 bell pepper (red or green), diced

- 1 small red onion, finely chopped
- 2 cloves garlic, minced
- 4 cups tomato juice
- 1/4 cup red wine vinegar
- 1/4 cup olive oil
- Salt and pepper to taste
- 1 teaspoon sugar
- Fresh basil or parsley for garnish

Directions:

1. In a blender or food processor, combine the chopped tomatoes, cucumber, bell pepper, red onion, and garlic. Blend until smooth.

2. Pour the mixture into a large bowl and add tomato juice, red wine vinegar, and olive oil. Mix well.

3. Season the gazpacho with salt, pepper, and sugar. Adjust the seasoning to suit your taste.

4. Cover the bowl and refrigerate for at least 2 hours to allow the flavors to meld and the soup to chill.

5. Before serving, give the gazpacho a good stir. Taste and adjust the seasoning if necessary.

6. Ladle the chilled gazpacho into bowls and garnish with fresh basil or parsley.

CHAPTER 3

TIMELESS MAIN COURSES

BEEF WELLINGTON

- *Serving Size: 6-8 servings*

- *Prep Time: 30 minutes*

- *Cooking Time: 25-30 minutes*

Nutrition Info: (Per serving, assuming 8 servings)

- Calories: 500
- Protein: 30g
- Fat: 35g
- Carbohydrates: 20g
- Fiber: 2g

Ingredients:

- 2 pounds beef tenderloin
- Salt and black pepper, to taste
- 2 tablespoons olive oil
- 1 pound mushrooms, finely chopped
- 4 cloves garlic, minced
- 1 tablespoon fresh thyme, chopped
- 2 tablespoons Dijon mustard

- **8-10 slices prosciutto**
- **1 pound puff pastry, thawed if frozen**
- **1 egg, beaten (for egg wash)**

Directions:

1. Season the beef with salt and pepper. Heat olive oil in a pan and sear the beef on all sides until browned. Let it cool.

2. In the same pan, sauté mushrooms, garlic, and thyme until the moisture evaporates. Allow it to cool, then mix in Dijon mustard.

3. Lay out prosciutto slices on plastic wrap, slightly overlapping. Spread the mushroom mixture on top.

4. Place the seared beef on the mushroom-covered prosciutto and roll it tightly, using the plastic wrap. Chill in the refrigerator.

5. Roll out puff pastry and unwrap the beef from the plastic. Wrap the pastry around the beef, sealing the edges. Brush with egg wash.

6. Bake at 400°F (200°C) for 25-30 minutes or until the pastry is golden brown. Let it rest for 10 minutes before slicing.

CHICKEN MARSALA

- *Serving Size: 4 servings*

- *Prep Time: 15 minutes*

- *Cooking Time: 20 minutes*

Nutrition Info (per serving):

- **Calories: 450**
- **Protein: 35g**
- **Fat: 18g**
- **Carbohydrates: 30g**
- **Fiber: 2g**
- **Sugar: 2g**

Ingredients:

- **4 boneless, skinless chicken breasts**
- **1 cup all-purpose flour, for dredging**
- **Salt and pepper to taste**
- **4 tablespoons olive oil**
- **8 oz mushrooms, sliced**
- **1/2 cup Marsala wine**
- **1/2 cup chicken broth**
- **2 tablespoons unsalted butter**
- **2 tablespoons fresh parsley, chopped**

Directions:

1. Begin by pounding the chicken breasts to an even thickness. Season with salt and pepper.

2. Dredge each chicken breast in flour, shaking off excess. This helps create a golden brown crust when cooking.

3. In a large skillet, heat 2 tablespoons of olive oil over medium-high heat. Add the chicken breasts and cook until golden brown on both sides, approximately 5 minutes per side. Remove the chicken and set aside.

4. In the same skillet, add the remaining 2 tablespoons of olive oil. Add the sliced mushrooms and sauté until they release their moisture and become golden brown.

5. Pour in the Marsala wine, scraping the bottom of the skillet to incorporate the flavorful bits. Let it simmer for a couple of minutes.

6. Add the chicken broth to the skillet and bring the mixture to a boil. Reduce the heat to low, return the chicken to the skillet, and let it simmer until the chicken is cooked through, about 5-7 minutes.

7. Stir in the butter and parsley, allowing the sauce to thicken. Adjust salt and pepper to taste.

8. Serve the Chicken Marsala over your favorite pasta or with mashed potatoes, spooning the flavorful mushroom sauce over the top.

LOBSTER THERMIDOR

- *Serving Size: This recipe yields 2-4 servings, depending on whether it's the main course or part of a multi-course meal.*

- *Cooking Time: Approximately 30 minutes.*

- *Prep Time: Plan for about 20 minutes to prepare the lobster and sauce.*

Nutrition Info (per serving, assuming 4 servings):

- **Calories: 550**
- **Protein: 30g**
- **Carbohydrates: 10g**
- **Fat: 42g**
- **Cholesterol: 200mg**
- **Sodium: 800mg**

Ingredients:

- **2 live lobsters (about 1.5 to 2 pounds each)**
- **1/4 cup unsalted butter**
- **1/4 cup all-purpose flour**
- **1 cup whole milk**
- **1/2 cup heavy cream**
- **1/2 cup grated Gruyere cheese**

- 1/4 cup grated Parmesan cheese
- 2 tablespoons Dijon mustard
- 2 tablespoons dry white wine
- 2 tablespoons chopped fresh parsley
- Salt and pepper to taste

Directions:

1. Prep the Lobsters: Boil the lobsters until they turn red, about 8-10 minutes. Let them cool, then crack the shells and remove the meat. Cut the lobster meat into bite-sized pieces.

2. Prepare the Sauce: In a saucepan, melt butter over medium heat. Stir in the flour to create a roux. Gradually whisk in the milk and heavy cream until the mixture thickens. Add Gruyere and Parmesan cheeses, stirring until melted. Season with salt and pepper.

3. Enhance the Flavor: Stir in Dijon mustard and white wine, then add the lobster meat to the sauce. Gently fold in the lobster until it is evenly coated.

4. Broil to Perfection: Preheat your broiler. Spoon the lobster mixture into lobster shells or a baking dish. Place under the broiler until the top is golden and bubbly, about 5-7 minutes.

5. Garnish and Serve: Sprinkle chopped parsley over the Lobster Thermidor for a burst of freshness. Serve immediately, and watch as your guests savor every delicious bite.

COQ AU VIN

- *Serving Size: 4 servings*

- *Prep Time: 20 minutes*

- *Cooking Time: 2 hours*

Nutrition Information (per serving):

- Calories: 500
- Protein: 35g
- Carbohydrates: 10g
- Fat: 25g
- Fiber: 2g

Ingredients:

- 1 whole chicken (about 3-4 pounds), cut into pieces
- 1 bottle (750ml) red wine (preferably a robust red like Burgundy)
- 4 slices bacon, chopped
- 1 onion, finely chopped
- 2 carrots, peeled and sliced
- 3 cloves garlic, minced
- 2 cups mushrooms, halved
- 2 tablespoons all-purpose flour
- 2 tablespoons tomato paste

- 2 cups chicken broth
- 1 bouquet garni (a bundle of fresh herbs like thyme, parsley, and bay leaves tied together)
- Salt and pepper to taste

Directions:

1. Marinate the Chicken: Place the chicken pieces in a bowl, pour the red wine over them, cover, and refrigerate for at least 4 hours or overnight. This imparts rich flavor to the meat.

2. Cook the Bacon: In a large, heavy-bottomed pot or Dutch oven, cook the chopped bacon over medium heat until crispy. Remove the bacon and set aside, leaving the rendered fat in the pot.

3. Brown the Chicken: Pat the marinated chicken pieces dry with paper towels. Season them with salt and pepper. In the same pot with bacon fat, brown the chicken on all sides. Remove and set aside.

4. Sauté Vegetables: In the same pot, add chopped onions, carrots, garlic, and mushrooms. Sauté until the vegetables are tender.

5. Add Flour and Tomato Paste: Sprinkle the flour over the vegetables and stir. Add the tomato paste and cook for another 2 minutes, stirring continuously.

6. Deglaze with Wine and Add Broth: Pour in the marinating wine, deglazing the pot by scraping up any browned bits. Add chicken broth and bring to a simmer.

7. Combine Ingredients: Return the browned chicken and crispy bacon to the pot. Add the bouquet garni for aromatic flavor.

8. Simmer: Cover the pot and let it simmer on low heat for about 1.5 to 2 hours, or until the chicken is tender and cooked through.

9. Serve: Remove the bouquet garni and serve the Coq au Vin hot, either over mashed potatoes, rice, or with crusty bread.

OSSO BUCO

- *Serving Size: This recipe serves 4.*

- *Prep Time: Approximately 20 minutes.*

- *Cooking Time: Allow for 2 hours of simmering.*

Nutrition Info (per serving):

- **Calories: 450**
- **Protein: 35g**
- **Fat: 25g**
- **Carbohydrates: 15g**

- Fiber: 3g

- 4 veal shanks, about 2 inches thick
- Salt and freshly ground black pepper
- All-purpose flour, for dredging
- 4 tablespoons olive oil
- 1 onion, finely chopped
- 2 carrots, finely chopped
- 2 celery stalks, finely chopped
- 3 garlic cloves, minced
- 1 cup dry white wine
- 1 can (28 ounces) crushed tomatoes
- 1 cup chicken broth
- 1 bay leaf
- 1 teaspoon dried thyme
- Gremolata (optional garnish): chopped fresh parsley, grated lemon zest, and minced garlic

Directions:

1. Prep the Veal: Season the veal shanks with salt and pepper, then dredge them in flour, shaking off excess.

2. Sear the Shanks: In a large, heavy-bottomed pot, heat the olive oil over medium-high heat. Sear the veal shanks until browned on all sides. Remove and set aside.

3. Sauté Vegetables: In the same pot, add chopped onion, carrots, celery, and garlic. Sauté until the vegetables are softened.

4. Deglaze with Wine: Pour in the white wine, scraping the browned bits from the bottom of the pot. Allow it to simmer until reduced by half.

5. Simmer with Tomatoes and Broth: Stir in crushed tomatoes, chicken broth, bay leaf, and dried thyme. Return the veal shanks to the pot. Bring to a simmer.

6. Braise the Veal: Cover the pot and reduce heat to low. Allow the Osso Buco to simmer for about 2 hours, or until the meat is tender and falling off the bone.

7. Prepare Gremolata (Optional): Mix chopped parsley, grated lemon zest, and minced garlic. Sprinkle over the Osso Buco just before serving.

SHRIMP SCAMPI

- *Serving Size: 4*

- *Prep Time: 15 minutes*

- *Cooking Time: 10 minutes*

- Calories: 480
  - Protein: 30g
  - Carbohydrates: 32g
  - Fiber: 2g
  - Sugars: 1g
  - Fat: 22g
  - Saturated Fat: 7g
  - Cholesterol: 215mg
  - Sodium: 540mg

Ingredients:

- 1 pound large shrimp, peeled and deveined
- 8 oz linguine or spaghetti
- 4 cloves garlic, minced
- 1/2 cup dry white wine
- 1/4 cup chicken broth
- 2 tablespoons fresh lemon juice
- 2 teaspoons lemon zest
- 1/2 teaspoon red pepper flakes (optional)
- Salt and pepper to taste
- 1/4 cup fresh parsley, chopped
- 3 tablespoons olive oil
- 2 tablespoons unsalted butter

Directions:

1. Prepare the Pasta:

- Cook the linguine or spaghetti according to package instructions. Drain and set aside.

2. Cook the Shrimp:
   - In a large skillet, heat olive oil over medium-high heat.
   - Add minced garlic and sauté for about 1 minute until fragrant.
   - Add the shrimp to the skillet, season with salt and pepper, and cook until they turn pink, usually 2-3 minutes per side. Remove shrimp from the skillet and set aside.

3. Prepare the Sauce:
   - In the same skillet, add white wine, chicken broth, lemon juice, lemon zest, and red pepper flakes (if using). Bring to a simmer and let it cook for 2-3 minutes, allowing the flavors to meld.

4. Combine and Finish:
   - Reduce the heat to low and stir in the butter until melted.
   - Add the cooked shrimp back to the skillet, tossing them in the sauce for 1-2 minutes until heated through.
   - Gently fold in the cooked pasta, ensuring it's well-coated in the flavorful sauce.

5. Serve:
   - Plate the Shrimp Scampi, garnish with chopped parsley, and serve immediately.

CHAPTER 4

SIDES AND ACCOMPANIMENTS

ROASTED GARLIC MASHED POTATOES

- *Serving Size: 4 servings*

- *Prep Time: 15 minutes*

- *Cooking Time: 1 hour*

Nutrition Info (per serving):

- Calories: 350
- Total Fat: 16g
- Saturated Fat: 10g
- Cholesterol: 45mg
- Sodium: 50mg
- Total Carbohydrates: 48g
- Dietary Fiber: 4g
- Sugars: 3g
- Protein: 6g

Ingredients:

- 2 lbs (about 4 large) russet potatoes, peeled and diced
- 1 head of garlic
- 1/2 cup unsalted butter

- 1 cup whole milk
- Salt and pepper to taste
- Chopped fresh chives for garnish (optional)

Directions:

1. Roasting Garlic:
   - Preheat your oven to 400°F (200°C).
   - Cut the top off the garlic head to expose the cloves.
   - Drizzle with olive oil, wrap it in foil, and roast for 40-45 minutes until cloves are golden and soft.
   - Squeeze the roasted garlic cloves out of their skins and set aside.

2. Cooking Potatoes:
   - Peel and dice potatoes into even chunks.
   - Place potatoes in a large pot, cover with cold water, and add a pinch of salt.
   - Bring to a boil and simmer until potatoes are fork-tender, about 15-20 minutes.

3. Mashing:
   - Drain potatoes and return them to the pot.
   - Mash potatoes using a potato masher or ricer for a smoother texture.

4. Adding Flavors:
   - In a small saucepan, heat butter and milk until the butter is melted.
   - Pour the warm butter and milk mixture over the mashed potatoes and stir until combined.

5. Roasted Garlic Magic:
   - Add the roasted garlic cloves to the mashed potatoes and mix well.
   - Season with salt and pepper to taste.

6. Serve:
   - Spoon the creamy roasted garlic mashed potatoes into a serving dish.
   - Garnish with chopped fresh chives if desired.

LEMON HERB QUINOA

- *Serving Size: 4 servings*

- *Cooking Time: 15-20 minutes*

- *Prep Time: 5 minutes*

Nutrition Info (per serving):

- **Calories: 200**
- **Protein: 8g**
- **Carbohydrates: 35g**
- **Fiber: 5g**
- **Fat: 5g**
- **Vitamin C: 20% DV**
- **Iron: 10% DV**

Ingredients:

- 1 cup quinoa, rinsed
- 2 cups vegetable broth
- Zest of 1 lemon
- Juice of 2 lemons
- 2 tablespoons olive oil
- 2 cloves garlic, minced
- 1 teaspoon dried thyme
- 1 teaspoon dried oregano
- Salt and pepper to taste
- Fresh parsley for garnish

Directions:

1. Rinse Quinoa:
   Start by rinsing 1 cup of quinoa under cold water to remove any bitter coating.

2. Cook Quinoa:
   In a saucepan, combine the rinsed quinoa and 2 cups of vegetable broth. Bring it to a boil, then reduce the heat, cover, and simmer for 15-20 minutes, or until the quinoa is cooked and the liquid is absorbed.

3. Prepare Lemon Mixture:
   In a small bowl, mix the lemon zest, lemon juice, olive oil, minced garlic, dried thyme, dried oregano, salt, and pepper. This flavorful mixture will be the heart of your lemon herb quinoa.

4. Fluff and Combine:

Once the quinoa is cooked, fluff it with a fork to separate the grains. Pour the prepared lemon mixture over the quinoa and gently toss to combine, ensuring every grain is infused with the vibrant flavors.

5. Garnish and Serve:

Garnish the lemon herb quinoa with fresh parsley for a burst of color and additional freshness. Serve it as a delightful side dish or a light, nutritious main course.

Nutritional Benefits:
- Quinoa provides a complete source of protein, essential amino acids, and dietary fiber.
- Lemon adds a zesty flavor while contributing vitamin C, promoting immune health.
- Olive oil offers healthy fats, and herbs like thyme and oregano bring antioxidants and aromatic notes.

SAUTEED SPINACH WITH GARLIC

- *Prep Time: 10 minutes*

- *Cooking Time: 5 minutes*

- *Serving Size: 4*

Nutrition Info (per serving):

- Calories: 80
- Total Fat: 7g
- Saturated Fat: 1g
- Cholesterol: 0mg
- Sodium: 150mg
- Total Carbohydrates: 4g
- Dietary Fiber: 2g
- Sugars: 0g
- Protein: 3g

Ingredients:

- 1 pound fresh spinach leaves, washed and stemmed
- 3 cloves garlic, minced
- 2 tablespoons olive oil
- Salt and pepper to taste
- Optional: red pepper flakes for a kick

Directions:

1. Prepare Spinach: Wash the spinach leaves thoroughly and remove the stems. Pat them dry with a clean kitchen towel or use a salad spinner.

2. Mince Garlic: Peel and mince the garlic cloves finely.

3. Heat Olive Oil: In a large skillet, heat olive oil over medium heat.

4. Saute Garlic: Add minced garlic to the heated oil and sauté for about 1-2 minutes until it becomes fragrant. Be cautious not to let it brown.

5. Add Spinach: Gradually add the spinach leaves to the skillet. Toss and stir continuously until the leaves wilt, which takes approximately 2-3 minutes.

6. Seasoning: Season the sautéed spinach with salt and pepper to taste. If you enjoy a bit of heat, sprinkle some red pepper flakes for an extra kick.

7. Serve: Once the spinach is wilted and well-cooked, transfer it to a serving dish. Serve immediately as a nutritious side dish or a standalone light meal.

Nutrition Note:
Sauteed spinach with garlic is a powerhouse of nutrients, providing an abundance of vitamins A and C, iron, and fiber. This quick and easy recipe is not only delicious but also a great way to incorporate healthy greens into your diet.

PARMESAN RISOTTO

- *Serving Size: 4 servings*

- *Cooking Time: Approximately 25-30 minutes*

- *Prep Time: 10 minutes*

- **Calories: 350**
- **Total Fat: 12g**
- **Saturated Fat: 6g**
- **Cholesterol: 25mg**
- **Sodium: 700mg**
- **Total Carbohydrates: 45g**
- **Dietary Fiber: 2g**
- **Sugars: 1g**
- **Protein: 14g**

Ingredients:

- **1 1/2 cups Arborio rice**
- **4 cups chicken or vegetable broth, kept warm**
- **1 cup dry white wine**
- **1 small onion, finely chopped**
- **2 cloves garlic, minced**
- **1/2 cup grated Parmesan cheese**
- **2 tablespoons unsalted butter**
- **Salt and pepper to taste**
- **Fresh parsley for garnish**

Directions:

1. Prepare the Ingredients:
    - Finely chop the onion and mince the garlic.
    - Grate the Parmesan cheese and set aside.

- Warm the chicken or vegetable broth in a separate pot over low heat.

2. Sauté Onions and Garlic:
   - In a large, deep skillet, heat a tablespoon of butter over medium heat.
   - Add the chopped onion and sauté until translucent, then add the minced garlic and cook for an additional minute.

3. Toast the Rice:
   - Add the Arborio rice to the skillet, stirring constantly until the rice is lightly toasted, about 2-3 minutes.

4. Deglaze with Wine:
   - Pour in the white wine, stirring continuously until it's mostly absorbed by the rice.

5. Add Broth, One Ladle at a Time:
   - Begin adding the warm broth one ladle at a time, stirring frequently. Allow each ladle to be absorbed before adding the next.

6. Continue Cooking:
   - Repeat the process until the rice is creamy and cooked to al dente texture, which usually takes about 18-20 minutes.

7. Finish with Parmesan and Butter:
   - Stir in the grated Parmesan cheese and remaining butter. Season with salt and pepper to taste.

8. Garnish and Serve:

- Remove from heat, garnish with fresh parsley, and let the risotto rest for a minute before serving.

9. Serve Warm:
   - Spoon the Parmesan risotto onto plates, ensuring a creamy consistency. Enjoy this classic Italian dish as a comforting main course or a delightful side.

GRILLED ASPARAGUS WITH BALSAMIC GLAZE

- *Serving Size: 4 servings*

- *Cooking Time: 10-12 minutes*

- *Prep Time: 10 minutes*

Nutrition Info (per serving):

- **Calories: 80**
- **Fat: 4g**
- **Carbohydrates: 10g**
- **Fiber: 4g**
- **Protein: 4g**

Ingredients:

- **1 bunch of fresh asparagus**
- **2 tablespoons olive oil**
- **Salt and pepper to taste**

- **1/4 cup balsamic vinegar**
- **1 tablespoon honey**
- **1 clove garlic, minced**

Directions:

1. Preheat the Grill: Preheat your grill to medium-high heat.

2. Prepare the Asparagus: Trim the tough ends off the asparagus spears. Toss them in a bowl with olive oil, salt, and pepper.

3. Grill the Asparagus: Place the asparagus spears on the preheated grill, making sure they are evenly spaced. Grill for 4-5 minutes, turning occasionally, until they are tender and slightly charred.

4. Make the Balsamic Glaze: While the asparagus is grilling, in a small saucepan, combine balsamic vinegar, honey, and minced garlic. Bring to a simmer over medium heat and let it cook for 5-7 minutes until the glaze thickens slightly.

5. Glaze the Asparagus: Once the asparagus is done, transfer it to a serving platter. Drizzle the balsamic glaze over the grilled asparagus.

6. Serve: Garnish with a sprinkle of freshly ground black pepper and serve immediately.

WILD RICE PILAF

- *Serving Size: Approximately 4 servings.*

- *Prep Time: 15 minutes.*

- *Cooking Time: 40-45 minutes.*

Nutrition Information (per serving):

- Calories: 250
- Protein: 5g
- Fat: 8g
- Carbohydrates: 40g
- Fiber: 4g

Ingredients:

- 1 cup wild rice
- 2 cups vegetable or chicken broth
- 1/2 cup finely chopped onion
- 1/2 cup diced celery
- 1/2 cup diced carrots
- 2 cloves garlic, minced
- 2 tablespoons olive oil
- 1/4 cup chopped fresh parsley
- Salt and pepper to taste

Directions:

1. Prepare the Wild Rice:
   - Rinse the wild rice under cold water to remove excess starch.
   - In a medium saucepan, combine the rinsed wild rice and broth. Bring to a boil, then reduce heat, cover, and simmer for 40-45 minutes or until the rice is tender and most of the liquid is absorbed.

2. Sauté Aromatics:
   - In a large skillet, heat olive oil over medium heat.
   - Add chopped onion, celery, carrots, and minced garlic. Sauté until vegetables are tender.

3. Combine and Flavor:
   - Once the wild rice is cooked, add it to the skillet with sautéed vegetables.
   - Stir in chopped parsley and season with salt and pepper to taste.

4. Serve:
   - Transfer the wild rice pilaf to a serving dish.
   - Garnish with additional fresh parsley if desired.

Made in the USA
Coppell, TX
31 May 2024

32980253R00030